To _____

From _____

Date _____

She opens her mouth with wisdom,
And on her tongue is the law of kindness.
She watches over the ways of her household,
And does not eat the bread of idleness.
Her children rise up and call her blessed.

Proverbs 31:26–28

Published in Nashville, Tennessee, by Thomas Nelson, Inc.

All Scripture quotations taken from the *Holy Bible, New King James Version.* Copyright © 1979, 1980, 1982, 1990, 1994 by Thomas Nelson, Inc.

Produced with the assistance of The Livingstone Corporation. Project staff includes Betsy Schmitt, Mary Ann Lackland, Paige Drygas, Rosalie Krusemark.

Devotions written by Mary Ann Lackland and Betsy Schmitt.

Many "You have taught me..." quotes written by Dixie Oliver.

Design and production by Que-Net Media™, Chicago

Library of Congress Cataloging-in-Publication Data

Kinkade, Thomas, 1958-

A mother's timeless wisdom : inspiration for your journey / Thomas Kinkade.

p. cm.

ISBN 0-7852-6372-1 (hardcover)

1. Mothers–Prayer-books and devotions–English. I. Title.

BV4529.18 .K56 2003

242–dc21

2002153547

Printed in the United States of America.

03 04 05 06 QWV 7 6 5 4 3 2 1

A MOTHER'S TIMELESS WISDOM

INSPIRATION *for* YOUR JOURNEY

FEATURING THE ARTWORK OF

THOMAS KINKADE

Publishers Since 1798

THOMAS NELSON PUBLISHERS®
a Division of Thomas Nelson, Inc.
Nashville

www.ThomasNelson.com

Thomas
Kinkade

Contents

Introduction

No matter what the personality type—whether it's the cookie-baking homemaker, the super-organized, on-the-go volunteer, the kind with the listening ear and ready advice, or some combination of all of these—our first teacher is our mother.

From her mouth, we learn wisdom. From her interactions with others, we learn kindness and gentleness. From her activities, we learn perseverance and the importance of hard work. We listen and we learn. We watch and we study. And the lessons we discover last a lifetime.

From our mothers, we learn that love is not just a sentimental feeling expressed on a card but rather a choice, an action, something that we give away rather than just take. We learn that friendship is more about being a friend, and we watch her enact this as she listens for hours to the heartbreak of a friend whose marriage just dissolved.

Our mothers teach us that it is not so important what we say we are but rather what we do when no one else is around. We learn that gentleness is an art that desperately needs reviving, and that attitude alone can often mean the difference between success and failure. We are taught that it's far better to make mistakes than never to try and that laughter is the best medicine.

We learn from our mothers that worry should be our last option and that forgiveness should be the first. We are taught the importance of treating both those in authority and those who serve us equally with respect.

There was never a written exam or a pop quiz to test what we learned from our mothers. Rather, the proof and the value of those childhood lessons only become evident in adulthood, through the choices we make, the relationships we forge, and in our own interactions with others. For some, the final exam on what our mothers taught comes as we pass on that same wisdom to our own children.

It may be that we have never taken the time to reflect on the lessons we've learned from our mothers. Let these devotional thoughts on the following pages help begin that process. It may be that we have never expressed our gratitude to our mothers for how they prepared us for life. Let this book be an offering of appreciation and thanks to that special woman. Let "her children rise up and call her blessed."

Love

Beloved, let us love one
another, for love is of God;
and everyone who loves is born
of God and knows God.

1 John 4:7

You have taught me that when a person feels
the least deserving of love is when that
love feels the best.

*M*any people give us a chance in life. It may be a high school coach who gave you the ball in the crucial game or a boss who gave you a lucky break on your first job out of college. Regardless of who they are in each of our lives, we never forget these people and the opportunities they gave us.

Yet while others may give us our lucky chance to prove ourselves, only moms can teach us the priceless value of a second chance when we have nothing to prove. Moms give an unequaled and unrivaled gift when they give their children a second chance. It's that opportunity to get it right despite our less-than-impressive track record. It's that unconditional acceptance despite our childlike ungratefulness. It's that love and understanding at the very moment we feel the most unlovable. What compels a mom to meet a hot-tempered kid after a family argument with a peace offering of warm homemade sugar cookies and cold milk? How could she still love me? we wonder. We're no closer to the answer as adults than we were as children. Whatever their secret is to having unconditional love for their kids, the Mom Union isn't telling. It's not so much that we don't appreciate a well-deserved promotion or opportunity. There's just something about the undeserved and unexpected that tastes especially sweet.

"All that the Father gives Me will come to Me, and the one who comes to Me I will by no means cast out."

John 6:37

This is love, not that we loved God, but that He loved us and sent His Son to be the propitiation for our sins.

1 John 4:10

You have taught me that sometimes I don't
feel loved until the crisis is over.

From a mother's perspective, her children's lives are never hopeless. Even when the well seems to have run dry, mothers are somehow able to draw from the deep waters of a special reserve to share hope with their children. Their assurance and certainty about God's plan for our lives seem to flow in abundance just about the time ours begins to trickle. From a mother's point of view, the sun will shine again for us—even if it has temporarily moved behind a storm cloud. It's those times, in the middle of life's raging storm, that we can often only feel the sting of the rain on our faces, and we steadily lose hope. We may struggle financially. We may tire of trying to have children without success. Or perhaps our marriage begins to wane. At those times, the howling winds of depression drown out the voice of promise, and we begin to despair. The swirling darkness of failure surrounds us, blocking our view of the sun. We try, but we cannot seem to move past our pain.

Yet even when things seem their darkest, mothers faithfully hold out hope for our future. They believe the unbelievable and envision the impossible for our sake. They shoulder the weight of God's promise high enough for us to catch a glimpse of it again. And once we do, we begin to see flashes of hope. The rain subsides. The winds die down. We can finally see what she was able to envision all along—the promise of healing for past hurts and hope for the future.

Now hope does not disappoint, because the love of God
has been poured out in our hearts by the Holy Spirit who
was given to us.

Romans 5:5

Be of good courage,
And He shall strengthen your heart,
All you who hope in the Lord.

Psalm 31:24

You have taught me that to see as God sees
is to look into the eyes of another person
and see someone God loves.

*W*hat would it be like to be God for a day, and who wouldn't give anything to find out? Imagine spending your day high in the heavens, peering down upon all of humanity. All powerful. All knowing. Able to control everything to your liking with one touch. I've often wondered what that would be like.

Yet my mother taught me that to see the world through God's eyes has little to do with God's position. God's lofty perspective is not what makes God who He is. Sure, He is high above and infinitely holy. However, God does not perceive us from afar, coldly analyzing our character. He does not glare down upon us in swift-tempered judgment. No, He is intimately among us, daily looking deep into our souls, past our human rough edges, past what we are to what we could be. He doesn't squint from His throne room in heaven in order to identify us on the streets of earth. His presence is very near us—as a lover would walk closely beside His beloved.

In her own way, my mother saw things in a way I could never see them. She consciously tried to see through God's eyes. While others were quick to gossip about those who struggled, casting instant judgment, she saw past the pretense and peered a little harder to focus on the human need. She saw past another's personal chaos and saw a glimmer of human potential. She saw purpose and a greater plan at work—even when everyone around only saw failure.

Beloved, if God so loved us, we also ought to love one another.

1 John 4:11

"Judge not, that you be not judged."

Matthew 7:1

You have taught me that love isn't about
finding the right person; it's about being
the right person!

Contrary to all those famous story lines from Hollywood scripts, true love is not about finding another person to complete us. My mom taught me that much. When I would complain about being the only single girl in the city, she would always respond the same way. "It's not about finding another person to complete you," she would say. "It's about finding out who you really are and then summoning the courage to be confident and content in that person's skin." After all, she believed, if we are not happy with who we are, then how can we expect anyone else to be? She taught me to appreciate the time and effort it takes to develop as an individual so I would know more what I needed to expect in a spouse. Without taking the time to reflect on our own character and exploring our emotions and feelings, what would we have to offer that person if we finally did meet "the one"?

How I often hated to admit it at the time, but she was right. Her encouragement to travel, take chances, be young, and be free created layers to my being and intricacy to my character. My mom knew that the starry-eyed little girl looking everywhere for Mr. Right, sizing up every date's "marriage potential," would soon grow into a woman who had earned her age and wisdom. And at just the right time, she knew, love would find me.

But those who seek the Lord shall not lack any good thing.

Psalm 34:10

And now abide faith, hope, love, these three; but the greatest of these is love.

1 Corinthians 13:13

You have taught me that love is often hard
to find—and so much easier to give.

When I think of my mother, I think of the time she spent in her garden. Her fingers mixing the soil with expertise, her hair held back from her face under the wide brim of a familiar straw hat. She taught me to appreciate the beauty in a parfait row of pink and white impatiens, the passion captured in a red hibiscus. The lazy tendrils of a cypress vine and bell-shaped blooms on sky-blue salvia. She made it look so easy. Despite the fact that her friends so often lauded her green thumb, her family knew better. It may have looked like it came naturally to her, but we knew how hard she worked at it, giving it the time and attention necessary to be able to enjoy the results.

In the same way, it seemed that love bloomed often and early in her garden, though not because she found it naturally growing there. Love rarely comes to us that way. These full blooms, perfected by her patience and accented by her devotion, resulted from her careful planting in the soils of our hearts. One by one, my mother planted seeds of love in those around her. She watered them until they grew strong. She cared for them in dry seasons. From her, I learned the way love begets love. She lavished her love upon others with such ease and received bouquets of love in return.

And remember the words of the Lord Jesus, that He said, "It is more blessed to give than to receive."

Acts 20:35

"Give, and it will be given to you: good measure, pressed down, shaken together, and running over will be put into your bosom. For with the same measure that you use, it will be measured back to you."

Luke 6:38

Friendship

A MOTHER'S TIMELESS WISDOM

Two are better than one,

Because they have a good reward

for their labor. For if they fall,

one will lift up his companion.

But woe to him who is

alone when he falls,

For he has no one to

help him up.

Ecclesiastes 4:9–10

You have taught me that when I feel sad, I
don't need a pick-me-up—but a friend
to help me up.

A Depression baby, my mom grew up making her way through the world with a steadfast eye on what truly matters in life—strong family ties, enduring friendships, love for God and for each other. As a child, she quickly learned that everything else in life is material and temporary. She grew into a strong, godly woman, a rock of strength in our family. Always ready with a word of encouragement or sage advice, my mom gave us a sense of stability that could weather any storm.

Her memory motivates me even today. Whenever I get depressed and feel tempted to eat myself into a sugar coma or shop my way into serious consumer debt—those are the times my mom's words ring in my ears: "Don't sit there feeling sorry for yourself. Do something about it!" As she taught me, those little pick-me-ups are the hollow indulgences we give ourselves in an attempt to feel better. As if a spoon, a pint of Rocky Road, and a really good tearjerker movie will do any lasting good. Instead, my mom taught me the value of sending the guests home early from a pity party and turning instead to a better method of soul therapy. She taught me how a talk with a trusted friend can do wonders. She showed me how the faithful love of family can shore up my weaknesses. When life hurts, and it often does, we go to friends and family. That's what she taught me. That lesson has served me well time and time again.

Now when Job's three friends heard of all this adversity that had come upon him, each one came from his own place... For they had made an appointment together to come and mourn with him, and to comfort him.

Job 2:11

God sets the solitary in families.

Psalm 68:6

You have taught me that some need a leader to follow; others need a friend to walk hand in hand.

My father had enough personality for all of us—a loud belly laugh and incomparable winsomeness. Since I was always a quiet type, people knew instantly I was my mother's son. A faithful member of the women's auxiliary, my mom rarely spoke a word in the meetings. However, she could always be counted on to help where she was needed. No, she was not the prominent leader; instead, she followed instructions well and dedicated herself to supporting those in the lead. My mom faithfully served behind the scenes to care for others' needs and to demonstrate God's love to those around her. She found her niche among those who served beside her, and better still, she kept a watchful eye on those who fell behind. She noticed those who got lost in the crowd. My mom had a special concern for the hurting in our neighborhood, church, and community. Had she been a leader out in front, she may have noticed, but not been able to attend to, those needs. As a follower, she was able to keep pace with the bedraggled and encourage them. She joined hands with the hurting, and God richly rewarded her. She taught me through her example that there is nothing shameful about being a follower. In fact, she convinced me of the importance of being a follower and my responsibility for those beside me.

We then who are strong ought to bear with the scruples
of the weak, and not to please ourselves.

Romans 15:1

Now we exhort you, brethren . . . comfort the fainthearted,
uphold the weak, be patient with all.

1 Thessalonians 5:14

*You have taught me that true friends look
past sad, mad, bad, and glad and
they see me.*

Having the best mom in the whole world is one thing. (And don't many of us believe that to be true?) Having the best mom in the world who is also your best friend is something else altogether. Mothers set the pace for our lives with what they teach us about friendships. If they demonstrate truth, we will learn to value honesty in a friend. If they exemplify loyalty, we will not settle for anything less in a relationship. Ideally, moms give us a sense for what a friend should be. Faithful. Caring. Compassionate. We learn what it means to choose true friends by seeing these traits demonstrated in their lives. And from them we learn that true friendship doesn't depend on our perfect behavior. No, even when we're less than perfect, far from perfect, mothers still love us.

And the truth is that we don't always fit the portrait of an ideal friend ourselves! We may wake up certain days feeling crabby, self-centered, fairly unlovable, or even critical and unforgiving of others. Fortunately, God has specifically equipped moms to deal with this. They remain faithful when we are not holding up our end of the relationship. They deal with our bad days. They stick with us through seasons of success and failure. They overlook our ingratitude. They remain patient and compassionate even when we ignore their life concerns and carry on selfishly about our personal woes. Mothers see their children for who they are . . . and they love them anyway. No wonder they set a high standard for what it means to be a friend. They are the definition of true friendship, and God's blessing to us is the privilege of calling them both "Mom" and "friend."

"Greater love has no one than this, than to lay down one's life for his friends."

John 15:13

A friend loves at all times,
And a brother is born for adversity.

Proverbs 17:17

You have taught me that one of the sweetest
sounds to a human ear is the sound of
one's own name when lovingly spoken
by a friend.

*I*t was the first gift she gave to me. And even though I don't recall the moment at all, I'm sure it was a tender moment—considering it was a long time in coming. I still carry the gift with me and use it dozens of times a day. After moving from home to college, from job to job, from state to state, I haven't lost it yet. It still hasn't worn out, and it's never broken.

My name. It was the first gift my mother gave me. My childhood memories are filled with the ways she spoke my name. I remember how she said my name to gently wake me and tell me the good news that it had snowed so hard that school was canceled. I remember all too often hearing her shout my full name—first, middle, and last—across the backyard, freezing my little heart in terror. And I remember years later, after I had moved away from home, the way her voice spoke my name over the phone, wishing me happy birthday—a voice now calling from the other coast and sounding a little softer, a little more tired.

And then a few months later, my father said my name with uncharacteristic seriousness—he didn't have to say more. It was then I knew I'd heard my name from my mother's lips for the last time. To this day, whenever I hear my name on the lips of someone I love, it sounds familiar. It sounds like home.

"Even to them I will give in My house
And within My walls a place and a name
Better than that of sons and daughters;
I will give them an everlasting name
That shall not be cut off."
    Isaiah 56:5

"See, I have inscribed you on the palms of My hands."
    Isaiah 49:16

You have taught me that the best old friend
is one you can call up after a year and
continue the same conversation.

*S*enior citizen slumber party. That's what they ought to call it. Instead, they enthusiastically refer to it as "The Reunion." Four high school friends, class of 1955. Each year they still get together for a long weekend to share pictures and swap stories, playing board games in their pajamas until midnight and eating themselves into oblivion. Although we give our mom a lot of good-nature ribbing about her youthful annual rendezvous, we're secretly amazed and maybe even a little envious. She is part of something very rare—an endearing bond that has withstood the yaw and pitch of the real stuff of life. Cross-country moves. Marriage. Divorce. Parenting and grandparenting thirty-six kids between them. In an age where families and spouses are considered disposable, my mother and her friends have taught me the value of long-term commitment. I suppose at any point this foursome could have called it off, saying it was too hard to keep in touch. I assume they had a number of opportunities to do so—as anyone in this busy world of ours does. However, from what I've seen through them, the significant payoff seems to be worth all the hard work. My mom has shown me what I want when I am her age. She's taught me what it takes to cultivate friendships. And she's even convinced me that senior citizen slumber parties are actually very fun!

Your faithfulness endures to all generations.

Psalm 119:90

Now also when I am old and grayheaded,
O God, do not forsake me,
Until I declare Your strength to this generation,
Your power to everyone who is to come.

Psalm 71:18

Character

A MOTHER'S TIMELESS WISDOM

Even a child is known
by his deeds,
Whether what he
does is pure and right.
Proverbs 20:11

You have taught me that you can tell a
lot about a person's character by the
way he acts when he thinks no one's
watching him.

*I*t probably wasn't the easiest path to take. There you were with two young children, a cart full of groceries, a list of to-dos yet to be done, and dinner to get on the table. That's when you realized that I had "helped myself" to some candy that was conveniently displayed in the checkout lane. "Stolen" would be a more accurate description, even for a four-year-old.

It would have been far easier to get in the car, drive away, and deal with me at home. After all, nobody knew about it, except for you and me. It was only a ten-cent candy bar. (Yes, at that time it was!) So what was the big deal? It probably happened all the time. But that's not how you saw it. You saw a teachable moment, and obviously, one that I have never forgotten.

You marched me right back into the store, where I not only had to return the candy to the cashier but also apologize to the store manager. I don't believe I have ever even been tempted to take something that didn't belong to me since. (I also don't think I have ever picked up that particular candy since then!)

But this lesson was more than teaching a four-year-old not to steal. This lesson was about integrity and choosing to behave in a manner pleasing to God, even if there's not a soul around to witness it. Although it wasn't apparent to me at the time and only became clearer as I got older, acting honorably and honestly in the small matters—like returning a stolen candy bar—translates into a code of behavior that governs the bigger issues. You don't cheat on your exams, your tax returns, or your spouse. You don't lie to your friends, your boss, or your children. You treat others with kindness, courtesy, and respect even if no one else is there.

All that from a ten-cent candy bar. Not a bad deal.

The fear of the Lord is to hate evil;
Pride and arrogance and the evil way
And the perverse mouth I hate.

Proverbs 8:13

The integrity of the upright will guide them,
But the perversity of the unfaithful will destroy them.

Proverbs 11:3

You have taught me that good luck seems to
happen most often to people who have
worked long and hard.

When my daughter started high school, she had one goal in mind—to make the top-performing band in the instrumental music department. So we signed her up for private music lessons. She entered every contest that came along. She participated in every extracurricular music activity to get as much playing time as possible. Each year audition time would come around, and I would pray for her and wait. Each year the list would go up, and her name would not be on it. Still, she kept working, practicing, playing, and finally, her senior year, she made it. She called me at work, and I could tell as soon as I picked up the phone and heard the triumph in her voice that she had achieved her goal.

My mother taught us early on the value of hard work. My parents, both schoolteachers, never had anything handed to them. They didn't come from wealthy families. They didn't know "the right people" or have the type of connections that parlayed into terrific opportunities. They simply did what they knew how to do. They worked hard, my dad at the same school for forty years; my mother, for twenty-five years, heading back into the workforce after we were in our teens. Hard work. It's not easy. It's not glamorous. But it provided a wonderful, secure life for my sisters and me.

It also helped when I got out of college and landed my first job as a reporter for a weekly newspaper. It wasn't my dream job. Far from it. But I did what I was taught to do. I worked hard, and I gradually worked my way onto the staff of the daily newspaper and into bigger and better assignments.

Now, it's my son's turn to begin learning that lesson. When he comes to find me, frustrated, after trying to master a song on his trombone, I tell him, "Keep practicing. You'll make it."

The soul of a lazy man desires, and has nothing;
But the soul of the diligent shall be made rich.

Proverbs 13:4

That you also aspire to lead a quiet life, to mind your own business, and to work with your own hands, as we commanded you, that you may walk properly toward those who are outside, and that you may lack nothing.

1 Thessalonians 4:11–12

You have taught me that sometimes the most courageous thing to do is not react.

*B*y nature, my mother is a warm, gregarious, friendly person. She enjoys meeting new people and finding out about their interests and their lives. As a friend, she is thoughtful, considerate, the first one to write a note of encouragement during tough times, the first one there to lend a hand in an emergency.

So it had to hurt. It had to hurt when the women in the neighborhood snubbed her. It had to hurt when she was not included in their morning coffee sessions or when their children often excluded us from play because their moms told them to. It had to hurt deeply.

But growing up, we never knew it. When we asked to invite our neighborhood friends to our birthday parties, she smiled and sent the invitations. When she ran into those same neighbors at the grocery store or outside the school, my mother always offered a warm greeting and asked about their families. And when my best friend, whose mom belonged to that clique, chose to go to another girl's birthday party instead of mine, she soothed my hurt feelings and told me to overlook it and to treat my friend as I always had.

I never knew anything about it until much later when, as an adult, I was telling my mom about my own situation with a neighbor. As I told her how hurt I was by this neighbor whom I considered a friend, but who no longer spoke to me, she smiled gently and told me her story. That's how I knew what to do—to not react, to not accuse, to offer love where and when I could, and to pray for that person.

My mother has many wonderful characteristics, but I had never really thought of her as courageous. Until that day. Then I knew.

In return for my love they are my accusers,
But I give myself to prayer.

Psalm 109:4

"But I say to you, love your enemies, bless those who curse you, do good to those who hate you, and pray for those who spitefully use you and persecute you."

Matthew 5:44

Thomas
Kinkade

You have taught me that if I ever wonder
    whether something is right or wrong—
    it's wrong.

I was at my friend's house when she suggested that we take a trip to Jay's Sweet Shop. Now what healthy, normal eight-year-old can resist a visit to the local candy store? The only problem was that Jay's Sweet Shop was located on the opposite side of a busy street that my parents had told me never to cross without an adult. That's when the rationalization process kicked in. I wasn't crossing the street by myself. My parents never said anything about not going to Jay's Sweet Shop. Nothing would happen. I would look both ways—twice.

I went. After we had purchased our fill of candy and scurried across the street, I felt elated. I had made it, and nothing had happened. No one would ever know.

That emotion was short-lived. As I went home and was asked the typical questions—"What did you do?" "Did you and Karen have fun?"—a gnawing, restless feeling began to grow in the pit of my stomach. At first, I attributed it to the generous amounts of candy we had consumed earlier. But I knew better. Finally, I could take it no more. I crawled into your lap and confessed the entire episode. I knew it was wrong to cross that street, wrong to disobey you, and wrong to hide it from you.

I don't remember what punishment I received for this infraction, but I do remember what you said. You told me that if there's ever a doubt in my mind whether something is wrong or not, trust that inner voice, the voice of the Holy Spirit, and know that it is wrong. That voice enabled me to say no when my girlfriends in high school invited me to their drinking parties. It helped me to walk away from situations where I felt uncomfortable.

Now, it's my constant prayer that my children will learn to listen to that voice and obey it on their own journey.

Woe to those who call evil good, and good evil;
Who put darkness for light, and light for darkness;
Who put bitter for sweet, and sweet for bitter!

Isaiah 5:20

Therefore, to him who knows to do good and does not do it, to him it is sin.

James 4:17

PYE CORNER
COTTAGE
WELCOME

Thomas
Kinkade

Day 15

You have taught me that if a person is old enough to make his or her own decisions, that person must be man or woman enough to accept the consequences.

When my older sister came home from college her freshman year, she announced that she wanted to get a job down at the Jersey shore, independent of the family, and work there for the summer. Wisely you said nothing as she scoured the papers and at last found a job working at an ice cream stand on the boardwalk.

I remember going to visit her with the family about a month later. You said nothing as she showed us the closet she called her room. You held your tongue when she talked about the long hours and the loneliness of her days off because she rarely had time to meet other kids her own age, and when she complained about the low wages, part of which she had to pay for her living expenses. You didn't say anything even though you knew. She had gotten what she wanted—independence—but at a high price. On the ride home, we knew also. Even though my younger sister and I still were under your roof, we knew one day we, too, would be held accountable for the decisions we made—just like my sister.

Every wise parent knows the value of having children learn to live with the consequences of their decisions. God did. He could have physically prevented Adam and Eve from eating the fruit of the tree of the knowledge of good and evil. But He didn't. Instead, He gave them the freedom of choosing for themselves—and of living with the consequences.

It may be painful. It often is. But you knew then, as I do now, that living with the consequences of our choices teaches us to think and choose more wisely.

As my eldest daughter prepares to leave home for college, I know I will have to do the same for her as you did for my sisters and me—graciously allow her to make her own choices and live with the consequences.

Then the Lord God took the man and put him in the garden of Eden to tend and keep it. And the Lord God commanded the man, saying, "Of every tree of the garden you may freely eat; but of the tree of the knowledge of good and evil you shall not eat, for in the day that you eat of it you shall surely die."

Genesis 2:15–17

Attitude

Be anxious for nothing,
but in everything by prayer and
supplication, with thanksgiving, let
your requests be made known to God;
and the peace of God, which surpasses
all understanding, will guard
your hearts and minds
through Christ Jesus.

Philippians 4:6-7

You have taught me to start the day smiling
at others and end it by laughing
at myself.

*A*s we gathered to celebrate your fiftieth wedding anniversary, I reflected on the legacy you have built over the years. There are many gifts you both have given to us, but among the gifts I treasure most are the gift of laughter and the gift of courtesy. When I look back on the times we have shared together as a family, laughter has always been a key ingredient. We laughed with each other; we laughed at our circumstances; and we laughed at ourselves. You taught me early on the importance of not taking myself so seriously that I couldn't see the humor or the light side to my situation. It has been a gift that has served me well and has helped me through those times when the job didn't work out, the move was harder than I had anticipated, or when the car, washing machine, and water heater all broke down in the same week.

You also taught me that the small courtesies were most important. I can still recite the litany of instructions we all received whenever we went to someone's house—Always remember to say please and thank you; always offer to help; always remember to be polite, especially to those who are older or younger than you. As you constantly reminded us, it takes so little effort to offer a smile, to say hello, or to simply say thank you, yet it means so much to that person. I saw it lived out in the countless kindnesses you passed along to others, whether it was the janitor at school, a colleague, or the store clerk.

Now as I look at my oldest child, I am satisfied that your legacy has been passed along to her as well. I see it in the way she has laughed as she recalls the time she flunked her driving test, in how she has responded on the job with a smile and a thank you, in how she treats those younger and older than herself.

You have taught us well.

Then our mouth was filled with laughter,

And our tongue with singing.

Then they said among the nations,

"The Lord has done great things for them."

Psalm 126:2

Let nothing be done through selfish ambition or conceit,
but in lowliness of mind let each esteem others better
than himself.

Philippians 2:3

Day 17

You have taught me that how we respond
to authority may be the truest test of
our maturity.

I wanted to quit. I wanted to storm out of the classroom, walk away, and never look at the face of that man again. In no uncertain terms, I wanted to let that teacher know exactly how I felt about him and his teaching methods. In all of my then-sixteen years of experience, I had never felt more humiliated, more inadequate, or more hurt from the verbal lambasting of a teacher than on that day.

When you walked through the door that afternoon, dog tired from your own day in the classroom, I let you know in one emotionally charged barrage that I was never going back into that classroom again. And you listened. You listened until I had spent all my adolescent outrage, and then you spoke. Quietly. Wisely. Rightly. "That man is your teacher. He is the authority in the classroom, and he deserves your respect. You may not like the manner in which he spoke to you, but have you really considered what he said to you?" Tough words. Harder to put into action.

So I put aside my hurt. I considered the constructive part of what he said to me that day and overlooked the destructive way in which he had said it. I prayed for the man, for my attitude, and for my relationship with him. And I walked back into the classroom, respectfully and willing to learn what I needed to from him.

Many years later, you ran into that man, long retired from the classroom. No doubt, the years had softened the memories of my time in his classroom (certainly he had forgotten that day!), but he told you then how much he enjoyed having me in his classroom and what a good student I had been. It makes me smile even now to think about it. But it also makes me thankful because I'm able to tell my own children about the importance of respecting those who are over them.

Let every soul be subject to the governing authorities. For there is no authority except from God, and the authorities that exist are appointed by God.

Romans 13:1

Obey those who rule over you, and be submissive, for they watch out for your souls, as those who must give account. Let them do so with joy and not with grief, for that would be unprofitable for you.

Hebrews 13:17

*You have taught me that people who never
made a mistake have never tried
anything new. They stay in their safe
little worlds and never really live life.*

When my high school junior came home from school one day and announced that she wanted to enroll in the Adventures Studies class at school the following year, I thought she had lost her mind. The class called for a rigorous and demanding schedule of weekend camping trips that included rock climbing, cave crawling, and wilderness hiking. At that time, her experience in camping was limited to one (maybe two) Girl Scout overnights, and her hiking experience involved walking to the local store. Rock climbing and caving? Forget it. These activities were not part of our family vernacular.

I was all prepared to dissuade her of this fantasy—You've never done this before; what if you can't do it? What if you fall and break something? Then I remembered. You never stopped me when I came home and decided I wanted to try out horseback riding or go out for the school musical. Or the time I wanted to apply for a high school summer journalism program in a city nearly one thousand miles away. I didn't know if I could do it. I didn't know if I would fail. Neither did you. But you encouraged me to try, so I did. Sometimes I failed. Sometimes I succeeded. I've never become an accomplished equestrian, but I have established a career using the skills I've developed as a writer.

More than that, I have learned it's okay to take risks, to try new things, to explore new places. If I didn't, I would have missed out on my one and only time appearing on stage as a dancer. Or covering my first parade and trying to find that unique angle that would make a great story, or becoming the first high school "correspondent" for our local newspaper.

So I took a deep breath and I smiled as I said to my enthusiastic daughter, "Go for it."

"Have I not commanded you? Be strong and of good courage; do not be afraid, nor be dismayed, for the Lord your God is with you wherever you go."

Joshua 1:9

For God has not given us a spirit of fear, but of power and of love and of a sound mind.

2 Timothy 1:7

You have taught me that the difference
between winning and losing is often
an inch of perseverance.

*S*he lost that day. Finished dead last, as a matter of fact. By the time my daughter made the final turn toward the finish line, the other runners were well off the track and already packing up their gear to leave. And I couldn't have been prouder of her. She finished the race. Even though it took every ounce of strength and determination in her twelve-year-old body, she crossed the line. I know it wasn't easy, and she sobbed as she collapsed into my arms at the end of the race, but she finished well.

Finishing is never easy, whether it's a race or a difficult class or an unsatisfying job. But my mother taught me that there was no other alternative. Quitting was not a word in our vocabulary. If we signed up to volunteer, and it turned into more of a hassle than it was worth, we stuck it out to the end of our commitment. If we ended up in a class with a difficult teacher, we learned how to adjust and get through it. And still later, if the job didn't work out exactly how we had hoped, we first tried to make the situation work. But we never quit. We finished. It's what my mother taught us.

It's what I hope to pass along to my children. I knew that running was not easy for my daughter. Math is a constant battle for my other daughter. And my son is challenged with anything new that comes his way. It is not easy to watch any of them struggle. Sometimes, quite frankly, it would be easier to let them quit. And after watching race after race when more often that not my daughter came in last, I was sorely tempted.

But in the end, finishing is winning. I have learned that you never lose if you are able to persevere in whatever situations come your way.

So you see, she really did win that day.

"Yet the righteous will hold to his way,
And he who has clean hands will be stronger and stronger."

Job 17:9

Therefore we also, since we are surrounded by so great a cloud of witnesses, let us lay aside every weight, and the sin which so easily ensnares us, and let us run with endurance the race that is set before us.

Hebrews 12:1

Thomas
Kinkade

You have taught me that gentleness is a lost art.

*G*entleness is not necessarily an adjective that readily comes to mind when I think about my family. As a group, we tend to be vocal, opinionated, and more prone to blow off steam than to sit down quietly and discuss the situation. That's not to say we don't eventually get to that point. But it's not our first mode of response.

Yet, there were those moments when the gentleness you brought to a particular situation was exactly what was needed most. I remember in particular the days after I brought home my first baby. The entire family (both sides) had come to visit, and I must admit, I wasn't coping particularly well. I didn't feel great; I sure didn't look great (my body did not automatically spring back to its pre-pregnancy shape as I had hoped); and I was overwhelmed by the daunting challenge of motherhood.

As the group decided to go out for an afternoon of shopping and left laughing and arguing over which store to go to first, I couldn't have felt more depressed. Gently, you led me outside, sat me down in the warm, sun-kissed breeze, and allowed me to cry. You sat by my side, and for what seemed like hours, you let me pour out all my emotions in one huge torrent of tears. You didn't say much. You didn't need to. Just knowing that you were by my side was enough.

I cried again when you returned home several days later. But I knew it was going to be okay. I was somehow going to figure out what it meant to be a mother. I would eventually get myself back in shape, and life would return to some semblance of normalcy. And it did. You told me it would.

So now when my daughter walks in the door and breaks down in tears because she blew it in her auditions at school, I know what to do. I summon my gentleness and I sit. And listen. And care. Just like you.

He will feed His flock like a shepherd;

He will gather the lambs with His arm,

And carry them in His bosom,

And gently lead those who are with young.

Isaiah 40:11

"Take My yoke upon you and learn from Me, for I am gentle and lowly in heart, and you will find rest for your souls."

Matthew 11:29

Wisdom

If any of you lacks wisdom,
let him ask of God, who gives to
all liberally and without reproach,
and it will be given to him.

James 1:5

You have taught me that acts of kindness
are gifts to be given to others—and then
readily forgotten by the giver.

I saw her do it a hundred times. She'd busy herself in the kitchen for hours at a time with the most delicious mix of aromas wafting up the stairs. Fresh lemon squares. Chicken casserole. Light, hot yeast rolls. I can picture the familiar scene in my mind. Counters littered with pots, pans, and measuring cups. My mom's cheeks flushed with activity and lightly floured, her apron loosely tied around her waistline. As children, my brother and I would reach for a bite of a lemon square, and she'd gently chide us away . . . No, these delicious treats were not for our family. The meal was for the new neighbor who had moved in next door. Where others simply noted a new addition to the neighborhood moving in, my mother saw a family in need of a hot meal instead of another supper from a sack.

Generosity came second nature to my mother. Other times, it was for the elderly lady at church who was homebound. The expectant mother in the PTA. The widow in her Sunday school class. No one asked her to do it. She just did. Without fanfare. Without calling attention to herself. Sometimes she'd even leave the basket on the porch without a card. I realized she didn't do it to be noticed—she did it because she enjoyed giving.

Just as no one had asked her to do these acts of kindness, so no one asked me to learn from her example. I just did.

He who has a generous eye will be blessed,
For he gives of his bread to the poor.

Proverbs 22:9

But a generous man devises generous things,
And by generosity he shall stand.

Isaiah 32:8

Thomas Kinkade

You have taught me that five of the most
powerful words are "go ahead and try it."

*T*he three most comforting words my mother ever spoke: "Welcome home, honey." The four most tempting words I ever heard her speak: "Homemade ice cream, anyone?" But the five most powerful words? They'd have to be my mother's admonition to me whenever I came upon a challenge I thought I could not do. "Go ahead and try it," she would say, her voice full of confidence. She didn't make any predictions as to the outcome, win or lose. She didn't hedge her bets. She just encouraged me to find out for myself—a potent formula for getting me one step closer to success.

Growing up, I adopted her words as my personal motto. Little League. Debate team tryouts. Even learning to drive my first stick shift. Later, I entered college. And law school. Instead of fearing the unknown, I learned to stride out and meet it regardless of success or failure. She believed in my God-given abilities and gave me confidence to exercise them as a means of finding out what I was "good at." She helped me to unearth the raw talents within me that I otherwise wouldn't have known I had. Now, when my own children come across the unknown in their young lives, I encourage and empower them with this same motherly maxim: "Go ahead and try it."

Brethren, I do not count myself to have apprehended; but one thing I do, forgetting those things which are behind and reaching forward to those things which are ahead, I press toward the goal for the prize of the upward call of God in Christ Jesus.

Philippians 3:13–14

"Fear not, for I have redeemed you;
I have called you by your name;
You are Mine."

Isaiah 43:1

You have taught me that a wise woman reflects
on her lack of wisdom, unlike the fool,
who assumes she already has it.

More. My mother taught me to want it. More from life. More from myself. Less complacency. Less compromise. Without her steady encouragement, I would have settled for good and the occasional better, instead of striving for God's very best. I was always a good Christian, a good wife, and good mother, yet life had begun to bore me. Was this all there was? Assuming I had already "arrived," I soon allowed laziness to creep into areas where I once thought I had it all together. The consequences of neglecting my soul—spending less and less time in prayer and study with God—were devastating. Less prayer eventually led to having less patience with my family, being less focused at work, and being less loving at home.

With the gentle, tender instruction only a mother can give, my mom addressed my need. She reminded me that a wise person knows she will never "arrive"— especially when it comes to the Christian life. Slacking off is dangerous. She pointed out there is always more to learn about being a disciple. More to know about Jesus Christ. More to read in His Word. Always more ways to apply His truth in our lives. When I began to exercise my mother's principle of "more," I grew excited about life again. I craved more of His Word and more fellowship with Him. Through my mother's willingness to speak into my life, God taught me the most about life when I least expected it.

Yes, if you cry out for discernment,
And lift up your voice for understanding,
If you seek her as silver,
And search for her as for hidden treasures;
Then you will understand the fear of the Lord,
And find the knowledge of God.

Proverbs 2:3–5

Pride goes before destruction,
And a haughty spirit before a fall.

Proverbs 16:18

*You have taught me that you can learn a lot
about a person by listening to how he
describes others.*

It's a mother thing, this uncanny ability to speak without saying a word. Yet for children of all ages, it's a universally recognizable phenomenon. It's a certain look. A subtle glance in our direction. It's lost on others, but we can read "the look" on our mothers' faces instantly. And we know what it means. Mothers communicate volumes without so much as a word or a whisper. And we just thought they had eyes in the backs of their heads! No, as we learn later in life, it's more complex than that. It takes discernment and above all, patient listening.

Over the years I came to appreciate the fact that my mother could perceive unspoken things about other people. She's an excellent judge of character—the best, in my opinion. I remember introducing new friends to my mom for the first time and watching her face to see if I could read her reaction. Mom picked up on so much just by listening—to how the girl described her family, her friends, others around her. And by watching my mother in those situations, I learned that a few minutes of good, uninterrupted listening can reveal an awful lot about another person—whether he or she has a critical and unforgiving heart, a generous and gracious spirit, an enthusiasm for life, a compassionate and genuine love for others.

And just as I tried to do with my mother, so I see my kids watching my face for a reaction. They're looking for that little look of warning or that warm glance of approval. All too often we think we know what a person is about, but we don't listen—at least not with a mother's ear. And, more often than not, heeding that first look from Mom turns out to be a wise decision.

The way of a fool is right in his own eyes
But he who heeds counsel is wise.

Proverbs 12:15

So then, my beloved brethren, let every man be swift to
hear, slow to speak, slow to wrath.

James 1:19

You have taught me that life is what is
happening while you're planning
your future.

When will I get married? And whom will I marry? Where will I live? What will I do? What is my purpose? These are questions mothers are supposed to answer for their children, right? At least I believed so as a child. Once I eagerly asked my mother about God's will for my life. I stood poised and ready to capture all the nuggets of wisdom she would share with me. "Sweetheart," she began slowly, "God's will is mostly about today, not tomorrow. So do the next thing today." This was not the answer I was looking for. In fact, I felt downright disappointed. Yet it was the very thing I needed to hear, despite my childlike frustration at the moment.

In time, I began to sense the wisdom in my mother's carefully chosen words. I even began to feel relieved, enlightened. You mean to tell me that God's will for my life is mostly about today? Not about some foreign future I can't even begin to see from here? What a relief! My mother taught me to simply focus on God's assigned portion for me today and then respond wholeheartedly. As a student, it meant going to school. As an older adult, it meant showing up for work every day. Honoring my husband. Even doing homework with my son. Through the ins and outs of life, I learned to appropriate my mother's valuable insight. If I was not willing to believe and act on God's will for me today, however mundane it may be, what good would it do to wonder about tomorrow?

"Therefore do not worry about tomorrow, for tomorrow will worry about its own things. Sufficient for the day is its own trouble."

Matthew 6:34

Teach me to do Your will,
For You are my God:
Your Spirit is good.
Lead me in the land of uprightness.

Psalm 143:10

You have taught me that being alone and being
lonely are not the same thing.

I used to think it was strange—my mom spending all her time alone in that big house in the country. Was she scared at night? What if she became sick? With the five-year anniversary of my dad's death coming up, my sisters and I debated the wisdom of her decision to keep the house. Maybe it's time for her to move in with one of us, we thought to ourselves After all, we couldn't bear the thought of her being lonely. We sat Mom down for a heart-to-heart family discussion. And we were surprised to find out that she wasn't the one who needed a different perspective; we were.

Mom helped us see that our concerns were unfounded assumptions. Mom was alone, certainly. And she missed my father immensely. But she was not lonely, and she wanted us to know the difference. After years of being a widow, she had come to know what the Bible describes as the "fellowship of Christ's sufferings"—a sweet kinship with Jesus that only comes through heartache. With Him, she was never lonely. Alone, yes. Yet not lonely.

As her child, I am grateful to God for the gift He has given my mother. A real sense of His presence. A companionship and contentedness that can only come from His hand. She has inspired me to pray for the same sense of God's presence in my own life as many times I can feel loneliness making its way into my thoughts. When that happens, I ask Jesus to be real to me so that even when I am alone, I can enjoy the warmth of His presence.

That I may know Him and the power of His resurrection, and the fellowship of His sufferings.

Philippians 3:10

"And the Lord, He is the One who goes before you. He will be with you, He will not leave you nor forsake you; do not fear nor be dismayed."

Deuteronomy 31:8

"Fear not, for I am with you;
Be not dismayed, for I am your God.
I will strengthen you,
Yes, I will help you,
I will uphold you with My righteous right hand."

Isaiah 41:10

Day 27

You have taught me to wait to worry.

*S*ome things are worth waiting for in life. A cab in the middle of a rainstorm. Slow-cooked barbeque. The love of a good man. The time to start worrying. It's that last one that really tries my patience.

Worry plagues us and robs us of our joy far too often, doesn't it? We tend to jump quickly to worrying without a second thought or a moment's delay. Just ask my mother. She'll be the first to admit that waiting to worry is the hardest discipline a person can undertake, yet she is also aware that the results are well worth it. As my mom says, worrying today rarely takes away any of tomorrow's heartache. All that worry is good for is sapping hope from today. Money troubles. Illness. Relationships. Work. Instead of relieving our sorrow, worry usually only diminishes our strength.

My mother has this uncanny ability to appear calm in the midst of a crisis. Whether or not she really feels calm inside is her trade secret, but her coolheadedness and wisdom are indispensable. Like water on a flame, watching her reaction douses my initial doubts and fears. When will I ever learn that most of what I worry about never comes true anyway? It doesn't take a prophet to know that. It just takes the gentle reminder of a mother who's been there, done that when it comes to most of the major hurdles in life. No matter how many times my mother told me to wait to worry, what really sank into my heart was her example time and time again. I'm still learning this lesson, Mom.

"Therefore I say to you, do not worry about your life, what you will eat or what you will drink; nor about your body, what you will put on. Is not life more than food and the body more than clothing?"

Matthew 6:25

"You will keep him in perfect peace,
Whose mind is stayed on You,
Because he trusts in You."

Isaiah 26:3

You have taught me that no matter how nice
a person seems to be, if she is rude to
a stranger, she will eventually act that
way toward you.

*R*espect. My mom taught me about the doors it opens when you use it. It keeps key relationships on track. It is essential to helping business negotiations run smoothly. She also taught me that the absence of respect speaks just as loudly as its presence. When this characteristic is missing in a person's life, it becomes glaringly apparent. Mom explained that respect is a consistent attitude and lifestyle—not a toggle switch between on and off. Ultimately, respect becomes second nature for those who follow Christ's example.

When it comes to establishing a healthy friendship, respect must flow between both parties. And it usually does with people who have a special affection for one another. But Mom insisted that genuine respect is not reserved just for special people. As a professional businesswoman, my mom's consistency in the way she treated everyone, from her secretary to her supervisor, made an impression on me early on in life. I saw my mom face dozens of opportunities that could have dissuaded her from treating others with dignity and worth. Like her, we may be ignored. We may be mistreated. We may even encounter someone who appears undeserving of our respect. However, Christ's rule is for us to treat all people respectfully out of reverence for Him. Without exception.

Honor all people. Love the brotherhood. Fear God.
Honor the king.

1 Peter 2:17

A gracious woman retains honor.

Proverbs 11:16

You have taught me to forgive as quickly as I can.

When I came home that night I cried in my mother's lap, hardly caring that I was wrinkling my carefully pressed shirt and ruining the makeup I had spent hours applying earlier for my date. It was my first real love and my first breakup. She smoothed my hair with her gentle hand and let me cry for a while as I sobbed to her about what a jerk the love of my life had turned out to be. However, instead of coddling me in my sorrow, she soon addressed the matter at hand. "The quicker you can forgive him, the quicker you'll get over this." Forgiveness seemed an eternity away at the moment. Why would I forgive him for hurting me? He was wrong! As if she could hear my thoughts, she shook her head knowingly and continued. "Forgiveness doesn't make what happened to you alright. It makes you alright. And if you forgive him now, you're going to be just fine."

Although it took me a while to believe the wisdom in her words, I eventually saw that she was right. Now that the days of young love and high school romances are long past, my mother's words still come to mind whenever I am tempted to hold a grudge against someone. "Forgive as quickly as you can." Refusing to forgive someone ends up hurting us instead of the other person. Longing to hold on to bitterness eats away at our peace, like an acid to our souls. My mother knew that forgiveness is a balm bringing healing to those who receive it and binding up our own wounds as well.

Bearing with one another, and forgiving one another, if anyone has a complaint against another; even as Christ forgave you, so you also must do.

Colossians 3:13

"And whenever you stand praying, if you have anything against anyone, forgive him, that your Father in heaven may also forgive you your trespasses."

Mark 11:25

You have taught me that people who are
successful have simply picked
themselves up one time more than
they were knocked down.

*I*t's impossible to glean diligence from books. Nor will an eloquent lecture teach us the concept. Diligence is rarely learned by precept; however, it is unforgettable once we've seen it in action. We must discover its benefits for ourselves. Finding a living model of persistence in a world spoiled by instant gratification is easier said than done. The idea of persisting through a magnificent series of defeats seems incomprehensible to a world that, on the whole, has yet to learn the payoff for persistence. However, most mothers are rich in the experience. Those who have lost a job, struggled in a marriage, or missed another promotion know the crossroads of commitment well. When the world would say, "Why continue trying?" mothers remind us, "Try we must!"

Mothers have a special interest in disturbing our complacency because they believe inertia is an ill fit for their children—especially a child of God. We must keep going. We must keep throwing ourselves into the task again. Why persist? Because diligence is never an end unto itself. It leads to layers of character and depth in our personality—forged, shaped, and polished by those times when we refused to quit. When we got back in the game. When we kept going despite fatigue and failure. Knowing by rote that one must persevere is one thing. However, living up to a mother's example of perseverance is quite another.

And not only that, but we also glory in tribulations, knowing that tribulation produces perseverance; and perseverance, character; and character, hope.

Romans 5:3–4

Therefore we do not lose heart. Even though our outward man is perishing, yet the inward man is being renewed day by day. For our light affliction, which is but for a moment, is working for us a far more exceeding and eternal weight of glory.

2 Corinthians 4:16–17

Words of wisdom...

Words of wisdom...

Words of wisdom...

Artwork by Thomas Kinkade used in A MOTHER'S TIMELESS WISDOM

Beyond Autumn Gate

Beyond Summer Gate

Blessings of Spring, The

Blossom Hill Church

Broadwater Bridge

Chandler's Cottage

Clocktower Cottage

Everett's Cottage

Foxglove Cottage

Glory of Evening

Glory of Morning

Hidden Cottage

Hidden Cottage II

Julianne's Cottage

Lamplight Village

Lilac Gazebo

Moonlight Cottage

A New Day Dawning

A Perfect Red Rose

Pye Corner Cottage

A Perfect Yellow Rose

Pools of Serenity

A Quiet Evening

The Rose Arbor Cottage

Rose Garden

Spring Gate

Stairway to Paradise

Stepping Stone Cottage

Sunday Outing

Weathervane Hutch

Victorian Garden